CREATIVE FASHION DRAWING

CREATIVE FASHION DRAWING

A COMPLETE GUIDE TO DESIGN AND ILLUSTRATION STYLES

NOEL CHAPMAN AND JUDITH CHEEK

Noel Chapman trained in fashion and textiles design. He is a consultant designer specializing in womenswear, knitwear, market, and creative intelligence, who works with a wide range of clients throughout Europe, the United States, and the Far East. Noel also writes on fashion-related subjects and lectures in fashion, textiles, and knitwear design. www.noelchapman.com

Judith Cheek trained in fashion design at St. Martins School of Art in London, UK, before specializing in illustration. She works with a wide range of clients across all levels of the industry, and her illustration work covers fashion, beauty, health and exercise, cooking, and food.

We would like to thank everyone who has so generously given their time and their work to this book, and to say a special thanks to Yvonne Deacon for her huge contribution and for freely sharing her thoughts and ideas. Without everyone's generosity, this book would never have happened.

Cover credits Front cover: Judith Cheek. Back cover, left: Yvonne Deacon; all other illustrations: Judith Cheek.

This edition first published in 2014 by Arcturus Publishing Limited

Distributed by Black Rabbit Books
P.O. Box 3263
Mankato
Minnesota MN 56002

Library of Congress Cataloging-in-Publication Data

Chapman, Noel.
 Creative fashion drawing / Noel Chapman and Judith Cheek.
   pages cm. -- (Creative workshop)
 Audience: Grade 4 to 12.
 Summary: "Instructs readers in basic methods for fashion design drawing"--Provided by publisher.
 Includes bibliographical references and index.
 ISBN 978-1-78212-412-2 (library binding)
 1. Fashion drawing--Technique--Juvenile literature. I. Cheek, Judith. II. Title.
 TT509.C523 2014
 741.6'72--dc23
                              2013004701

Printed in the USA

SL003587US
Supplier 02, Date 0114, Print Run 3389

CONTENTS

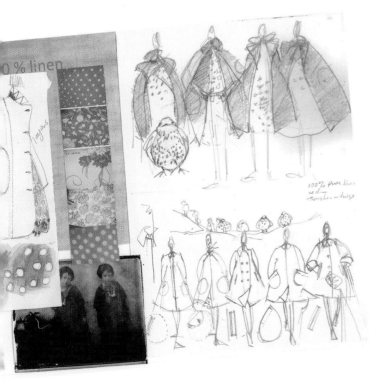

INTRODUCTION

This book is aimed both at designers who want to brush up their fashion drawing and illustration skills, and at would-be designers who want to learn how to draw and illustrate fashion from scratch. It is about learning how to draw fashion ideas better—how to record and develop your ideas, whether for your own enjoyment or in order to help you on your way toward a career in the industry, where being able to draw and record fashion is a real advantage.

What does the design process involve? What do we mean by inspiration and research, and which comes first? And how do drawing and illustration fit into this puzzle? These are some of the questions this book aims to answer as it charts the processes and activities of fashion drawing and designing.

Whatever the particular discipline of the designer—and arguably, of the artist, too—the need to draw reasonably well is most important, despite the popular if naïve opinion to the contrary. However, what qualifies as a drawing, and particularly a fashion drawing, depends very much on the individual and whether or not the drawing does the job it is intended to do. It is here that we may meet with some confusion: What is the difference between fashion drawing and fashion illustration? To put it simply, fashion drawing is what designers do first to record and develop their design ideas, and second, it conveys those ideas to others, for example, to the machinists and factory workers who will be making the garments. A fashion illustration is often commissioned by a fashion designer, a magazine, or perhaps by a PR team to convey the ideas of the designer. It may be intended to communicate something bigger than the clothes—the concept of the collection or perhaps the idea or desired image of the designer's brand. This idea or image may encompass all kinds of intangibles. For instance, it could be the task of the artist to express an attitude or a perfume, and so while the illustration may break many of the rules of fashion drawing per se, it provides a medium through which a designer may express their ideas. Regardless of the reasoning behind the fashion drawing or fashion illustration, the result needs to fulfill the brief.

Let's start by considering fashion drawing, which is the art of rendering the human figure, clothes, and accessories in an attractive and accessible way. To understand the processes and reasoning behind drawing fashion, it is important to appreciate the stages that a designer may go through in the course of the creative journey.

The designer may have an idea and will need to record that idea—to draw it effectively and sketch it on paper before it gets away. That idea then needs to be developed and refined, which usually involves a process of redrawing, of questioning, and of evaluation. Does the image depict what I was thinking about or trying to express? Are the proportions good? Is the silhouette right? Are the details correct and in the right place? Does the color balance work? The cutting and construction of the garment are also part of the design ethos and require thought and attention. These are just a few of the many assessments that need to be made, all of which will contribute to the successful realization of the design. Both the idea and the final outcome may evolve dramatically from the first sketches—perhaps with some surprises—and the processes of drawing and design are inseparably entwined.

Neil Greer
This digitally produced artwork was hand-drawn using a pen and tablet and the computer program Painter.

Rosalyn Kennedy
Client: *Bruce Oldfield*
Brush pen and pastel on colored Ingres paper.

Katharina Gulde
Client: *ONLY Bestseller*
Hand and digital drawing combined.

This book will guide you through a series of tutorials and aims to help you create better, more professional drawings. It will also attempt to encourage your own personality to shine through by showing you different possibilities across a range of media, techniques, and styles.

We will talk about equipment and materials, from the most elementary to a range of more specialist media, but first of all, you need to be able to draw by hand. In order to do this, we reveal how to draw a model: the human figure—static, posed, and in movement—which will later be dressed. This is always the starting point, and we will examine in detail how to accurately depict proportions and details such as hands, feet, heads, hair, and faces. It is important to point out at this stage that choosing the styling and look of a drawn figure is just like selecting a live model for real garments; the look and attitude have got to be right for overall success, because the wrong model with the wrong hairstyle and look will not wear the designs well.

Next, we discuss the usefulness of keeping and using a sketchbook, to gain inspiration from others' work and "found images" and materials, as well

as providing a collection of our own images from which we can draw on to piece final ideas together. We will also look at how to draw different fabrics, focusing on their surfaces and qualities, such as whether they are tweedy and chunky or fluid and floaty and so on. It is then possible to plot the designs of the clothes on the figure, getting the silhouette, fit, and proportions correct before moving on to the finer points, such as styling and construction lines, and how to draw pockets, collars, stitching, and other details.

Once the design has been refined, the drawing as an artwork needs to be completed with the addition of color, texture, and pattern. When broken down into steps, this process becomes clearer and more straightforward. Once mastered, these skills will enable you to draw with ease any design that your imagination may conjure up.

Throughout the book, we show a variety of contemporary fashion drawings and illustrations by an international range of designers and artists. This is intended to inspire you and to demonstrate the fabulous range of possible styles, all of which make up a handy reference for your own work.

CHAPTER 1

EQUIPMENT AND MATERIALS

Ask any designer what materials and equipment they need to draw and design, and you will get a variety of different answers. However, many will suggest that you start with a few simple pencils and some ordinary paper. This is fine initially, but as any designer will confirm, you will soon begin to favor certain types and brands, both for the way they perform and the marks they make and also how they feel in your hand. The size and shape of your hand, the speed and size at which you draw, and how hard you press all have an influence on your choice of implement, and this is before we even begin to consider the effect you wish to achieve in the actual drawing. Similarly, designers often prefer particular sketchbooks, whether they are large or small, landscape or portrait, spiral-bound, sewn, or concertina types. This section aims to reveal the choices on offer and the attributes and benefits of the different types.

YOUR WORKSPACE

While a sketchbook is something you probably use anywhere, including out and about, it is also a good idea to have a dedicated work area—somewhere organized to suit your needs and boost efficiency. It should also have a good natural light source, if possible by a window, and ideally have a movable work lamp fitted with a daylight bulb (full spectrum light) for more accurate color work. This space should offer you a place in which you can concentrate, where you have everything you need at hand, and where you can safely leave projects out without them being disturbed.

A desk or table that is steady and a comfortable chair with good back support are very important. Many designers like to draw on an angled surface. This does not need to be a sophisticated system—it could simply be a drawing board propped up at the back on a block or a small pile of books or magazines. A wooden 16 in. x 21 in. (40 cm × 53 cm) drawing board is best since it is manageable but has a sufficiently large surface area.

Photograph by Anne-Marie Ward

BASIC EQUIPMENT AND MATERIALS

While a designer may be perfectly happy with little more than an average pen or pencil and a stack of bulk paper, that is rarely enough for a good illustrator, who will usually carry a range of lead and colored pencils, various pens, lots of types of paper, and several adhesives. All the following usage descriptions are based on manufacturers' guidelines, but you can and should experiment, mixing as many together as you like.

HOLDING A PEN OR PENCIL

Before we look at the different types of materials, it is vital that a distinction is made between the right and wrong ways to hold a pencil or pen. It may sound dogmatic, but thousands of years of experience have shown that holding a drawing implement in a certain way does produce better results, so it is worth persevering to correct your technique, and if necessary, relearn altogether.

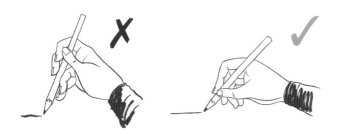

BASIC EQUIPMENT

• Pencils are graded from hard to soft, with H being hard and B soft. Both types are graded by number, with the highest being the hardest and the lowest the softest in the H range and vice versa in the B range. Choose a few different types and experiment. Automatic and clutch pencils, which contain an internal lead core that can be wound up and down, are also available with different grades of lead. These are very useful for getting ideas down quickly and cleanly, as well as being easy to use and maintain as you don't need a pencil sharpener. They are a little more expensive than standard pencils but are invaluable when you are out and about.

• Colored pencil crayons come in a good selection of hues and are either plain or water-soluble, with the latter giving a softer, more smudgy effect. As with

anything, the quality varies, and you get what you pay for, but a good start would be a basic selection box or carton of around 20 or so colors that you can add to as required. You need to look after pencil crayons—try not to drop them or shake them around too much because the leads will break inside. If you plan to carry them around with you, keep them in the box they came in or in a snug-fitting container.

• Ballpoint and rollerball pens are available in an ever-greater range, including those with gel inks, which are easy to obtain and use. As with all drawing implements, choose ones that are comfortable to hold and work with. It is worth trying out a few in an art store before purchasing one.

• Fine felt-tip or fine-liner pens range from the finest 0.05 mm nib to a thick 0.8 mm nib and are great for technical drawing as well as for general drawing. The variety is huge, and your decision will be based on the effect you are hoping to achieve. Some give a very clean graphic look while others are more fluid, and different brands vary, too. They are either water-based or permanent.

• Brush pens enable an illustrator to create very fluid lines in a variety of thicknesses, giving the swift, deft, expressive line you get from a paintbrush but with the cleanness and convenience of a felt-tip pen. Both brush and felt-tip pens are useful for adding texture to fashion drawings when trying to depict different fabrics.

• A stapler and adhesives such as masking tape, clear tape, and double-sided tape are required for masking areas of drawings, joining and fixing layers, and combining materials.

• Glue sticks are useful for adding elements such as scraps of materials and so on to sketchbooks.

• Bulk paper is available cheaply in different qualities, mostly graded according to weight. Letter size at 20 lb. (75 gsm) is a good basic paper. Sketchbooks vary according to paper quality and size; a standard letter-size sketchbook will generally suffice, although those who prefer more space should go for a larger ledger size. A small pocket sketchbook is a must when traveling around. For more about paper, see page 14.

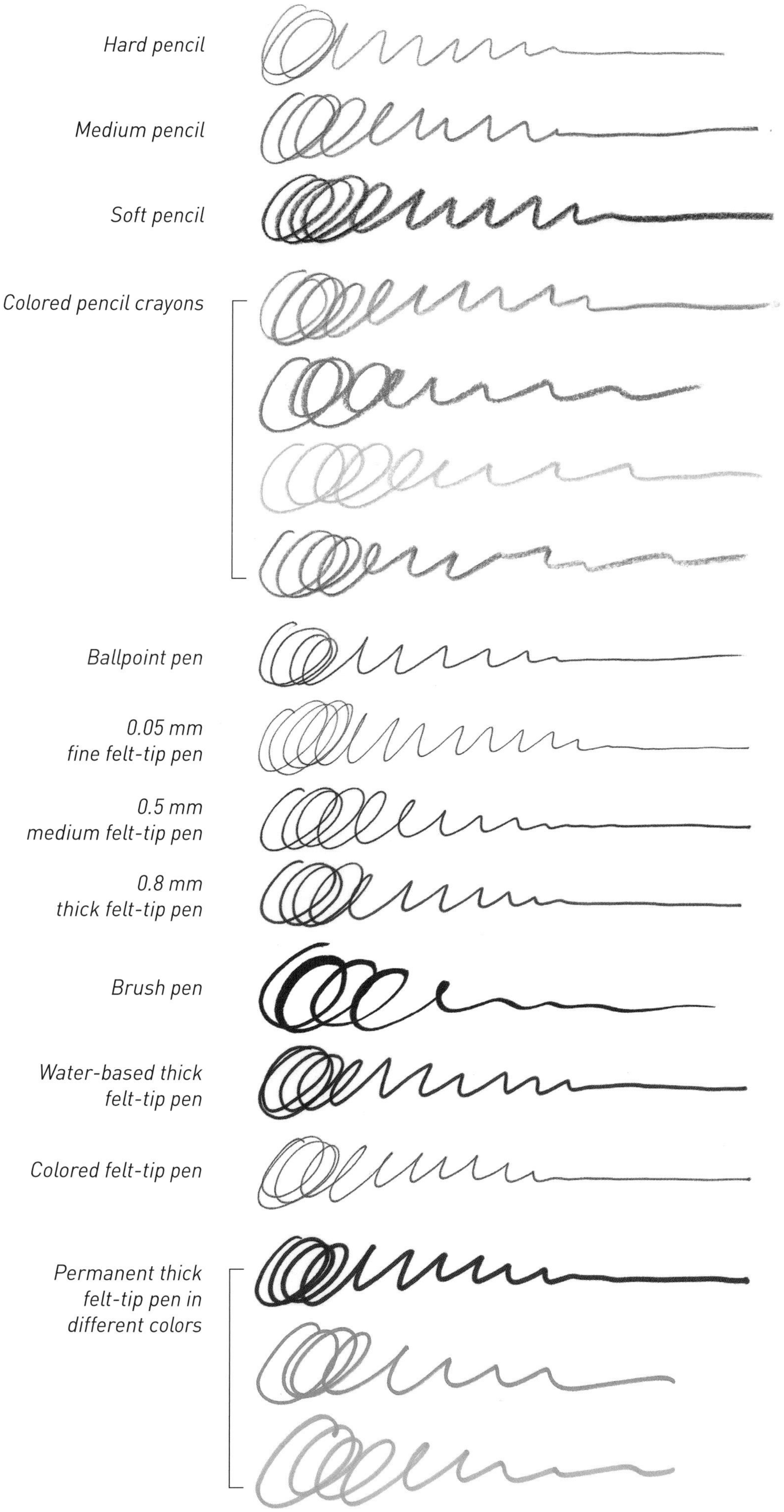

Hard pencil

Medium pencil

Soft pencil

Colored pencil crayons

Ballpoint pen

0.05 mm
fine felt-tip pen

0.5 mm
medium felt-tip pen

0.8 mm
thick felt-tip pen

Brush pen

Water-based thick
felt-tip pen

Colored felt-tip pen

Permanent thick
felt-tip pen in
different colors

BUILDING UP YOUR KIT: EXPERIMENTAL AND SPECIALIST

Once you've got the hang of some basic skills and are more confident, you can build your range of techniques by experimenting with a broader spectrum of specialist implements. These are termed "dry" or "wet." In addition, there are numerous types of paper that can be explored, producing a range of different finishes.

DRY MATERIALS

- Graphite pencils come in a huge range, from hard leads that give a very fine, faint line, to dark and soft leads that can be smudged with a finger and produce a rougher, more fluid line.
- China markers are waxy and make a bold mark on any surface.
- Conté pencils are very hard pastel crayons with which a variety of effects can be achieved, from very soft to dark and smudgy marks.
- Charcoal pencils are essentially charcoal in a pencil form, which means that they are not as messy to use as lump charcoal. Various grades of charcoal can be bought in this form. It is very fluid, and an extreme variety of lines and marks can be achieved— from the very soft and subtle to dark and bold scribbles—all of which can be easily smudged.
- Chalk pastels are either soft or hard. Pigment is bound together with clay and gum arabic, and as with paints, their price reflects the amount of pure pigment they contain. The first three saturations, containing the most pigment, are the most expensive, and as more white is added to make them paler, so the price reduces. Since they are expensive, it is worth trying just one or two to see if it is a medium you want to use. Soft and subtle effects can be achieved by overlaying, smudging, and blending colors.

- Oil pastels comprise pigment bound together with beeswax or mineral wax and nondrying petroleum jelly. They are very waxy and produce a bold, textured line that is excellent for quick life studies. Another feature of these pastels is they can be used to block in large areas of color and then blended to a flatter color using lighter fuel, mineral spirits, or turpentine.

WET MATERIALS

- Permanent marker pens are available in a fantastic range of colors. Each pen usually has two different-sized nibs, making them a versatile, clean, and quick way of putting down flat color.
- Watercolors are blocks of pigment bound together with gum arabic, glycerin, resin, and sugar. Water is applied with a brush, and the paint can then be transferred to paper to give bold washes of color; or you can build up layers of color in a tonal way. Once dry, subsequent layers of color can be added on top.
- Colored and black inks are essentially concentrated watercolors and are used in much the same way. They produce very intense colors, which is especially useful if illustrations are going to be reproduced. They can be applied with a brush to create washes of color or with a pen to produce a lively, scratchy line or to add finer details.
- Gouache, sometimes called designers' gouache, is an opaque water-based paint that is used for laying down flat color.
- Fixative spray is used for fixing pencil, crayon, charcoal, and pastel when a drawing is complete.
- Spray mount adhesive is essential for mounting work flat. Make sure you use it in a well-ventilated room to avoid a buildup of fumes.

DRY MATERIALS

Graphite

China marker

Conté pencil

Charcoal pencil

Chalk pastel blended with finger

Oil pastel blended with mineral spirits

WET MATERIALS

Calligraphy pen and ink

Marker pen using a broad nib

Marker pen using a fine nib

Watercolor over masking fluid

Concentrated pigment drawing ink over wax crayon (wax resist)

Gouache

PAPER

• Basic bulk paper is invaluable for sketching out ideas in rough. Printer paper is normally available in letter and ledger sizes and often has a weight of around 20 lb. (75 gsm). The most economical way of buying it is in reams (packs of 500 sheets) from office suppliers.

• Newsprint paper is thinner than printer paper and is semitransparent. You can work through a series of roughs, amending an image by putting another sheet over the top and redrawing and adjusting it until you get your "finished rough." The easiest way to do this is to buy the paper as a pad and begin at the back, working toward the front. Permanent markers and felt-tip pens will bleed through to the sheet underneath, so be aware of this. Many designers insert a sheet of heavier paper beneath their drawing page for protection.

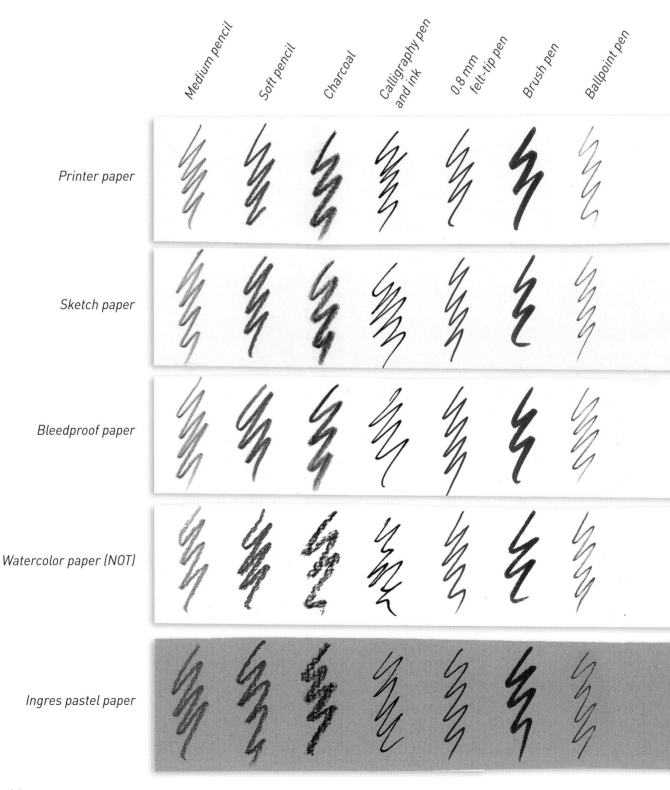

- Sketch paper is heavier and better quality than printer paper or newsprint and can be used with various mediums. It is an economical choice if you want to experiment with ways of putting down color. It is available in sketchbook form in many sizes and as separate sheets.
- Bleedproof or grafitti paper is for use with permanent marker pens and enables you to lay down flat color with a clean edge. Although you can use marker pens on any paper, they can appear dark and streaky, giving a soft, blurred edge, so bleedproof paper is the best choice if you want a crisp, reliable result. Alternatives include the heavier-weight Paris bleedproof paper and Bristol board—a smooth, double-faced paper that can be used on either side. It is best to use heavier-weight paper if the finished drawing is for your portfolio because thinner types start to look shabby very quickly. Thinner ones are fine for artwork that is going to print.
- Watercolor paper is generally used with watercolor paints and colored inks. It is available in three forms: "cold press" (called NOT), which has a rough-textured surface and is good for transparent washes and inks; a still rougher version (called ROUGH); and "hot press" (HP), which has a smoother finish and is better for use with opaque paints such as gouache. All watercolor paper comes in various textures and weights. Experiment to find the ones you like.
- Ingres paper is designed for pastel work, gouache, or collage. It is a beautiful, textured laid paper that takes its name from the neoclassical French painter who favored it.
- In addition to paper that you can buy, you can use scraps of paper torn from magazines, or you can start a collection of textured and colored papers for collage work or more experimental drawings.

ADDITIONAL EQUIPMENT

- Light boxes are useful but not always essential if you prefer to work directly onto your drawing paper. If, however, you want to draw a rough first, you can then attach it to a light box, place a fresh sheet of paper over the top, and trace the rough. You can easily see if this method works for you by attaching a rough drawing to a brightly lit window with masking tape, then placing another piece of paper over this and tracing the image.
- A computer, printer, and scanner, while not essential, do provide extra scope and can be beneficial. There are many ways to digitally enhance hand-drawn images, such as adding color and texture, changing the scale of a scanned drawing, combining multiple drawings, or creating collages by inserting photographs, images, and text. However, you should always keep in mind that: "*. . . these methods do not improve creativity and should only be used as tools to extend ideas . . .*" (Patrick Morgan).

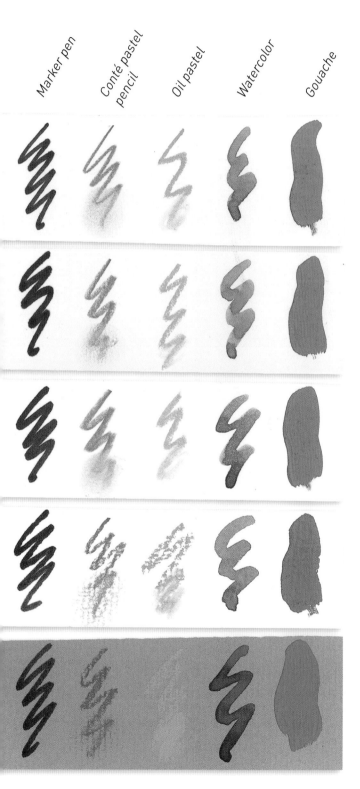

Marker pen   Conté pastel pencil   Oil pastel   Watercolor   Gouache

CHAPTER 2

ANATOMY AND POSES

The first step when drawing fashion is to develop a figure—a model that will wear your designs. You may end up with a range of characters that is constantly evolving, but when starting out, it is best to perfect one very basic form that you can adapt to suit different purposes. In this section, we will examine in detail how to get the proportions right for males and females of all ages; how to draw different poses, both static and dynamic; and how to accurately depict details such as hands, feet, heads, hair, and faces.

Once you have perfected these skills and achieved a physiologically accurate figure, it is important to allow your individual style to develop. This chapter contains a wide range of different examples across a mix of styles that should provide inspiration for you to experiment with your own ideas. It is easy to personalize the figure by varying the skin tone, hair, makeup, and so on, and you should try lots of options. Choosing the styling and look of your drawn figure is just like choosing a live model for real garments; the look and attitude has got to be right for the overall success of the illustration.

Once you've perfected it, this template can be placed underneath a drawing sheet, and you can loosely trace the shape of the figure. In addition, you can reduce or enlarge the size of the figure on a photocopier or computer so that it can be used for drawings of almost any scale, as well as replicating the many forms that can be used to depict a fashion collection.

PROPORTIONS OF THE FASHION FIGURE

All fashion artists apply a certain amount of creative license to the proportions of a drawn figure—some more so than others. This is because elongating a figure enhances the appeal of the design. The extent of the exaggeration can depend of the final outcome and purpose of the piece, but a fairly standard female fashion figure is seven and a half to eight and a half heads tall, and a male form is around nine heads tall.

It helps when drawing a figure to think of it as a human body, envisaging the skeleton that supports it, the organs it encases and protects, how and where it bends and twists, the joints and muscles that enable those movements, and the distribution of weight and how that shifts as the body moves. It is equally helpful to consider the physical space that the body occupies and how perspective affects our view of that space. Taking life-drawing classes can be hugely advantageous since it will expand your knowledge and experience of drawing the human form and probably enable you to try out a range of media, too. As with anything, practice makes perfect.

These sketches show a simple static pose and demonstrate how a stylish figure can be drafted using heads as a measurement guide.

Note the characteristic differences that define a male and female form: the female figure has narrower, sloping shoulders, a smaller waist, and larger hips (approximately the same as the shoulder width) than the male. Her bust is rounder and placed about midway above the waistline, while the neck and limbs are slimmer and less muscular. The male figure, on the other hand, has shoulders that are wider than his hips, a thicker and perhaps shorter neck, and his

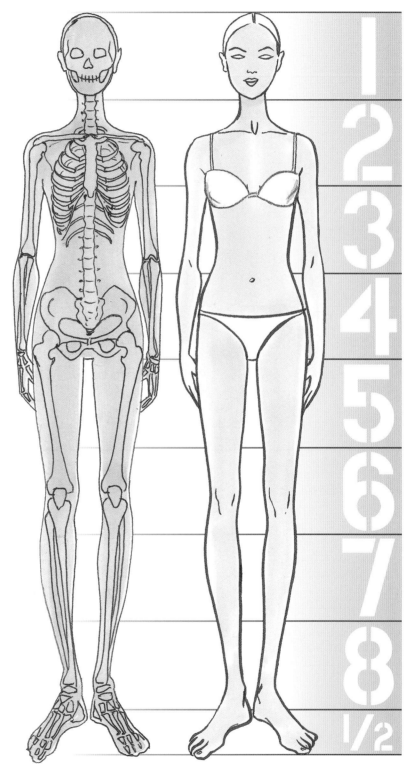

body is proportionately a little longer, which results in a lower waistline and a more square-shaped chest that sits a little higher than midway above the waist. The limbs are heavier and generally a little more muscular, and larger feet plant him more firmly on the ground. Many designers and illustrators often struggle at first to draw male figures that look convincing yet stylish, but with practice, this can be mastered.

This straight-on pose is the simplest to draw, and it allows numerous easy options for arm positions. It is clear and simple to "dress" in garments.

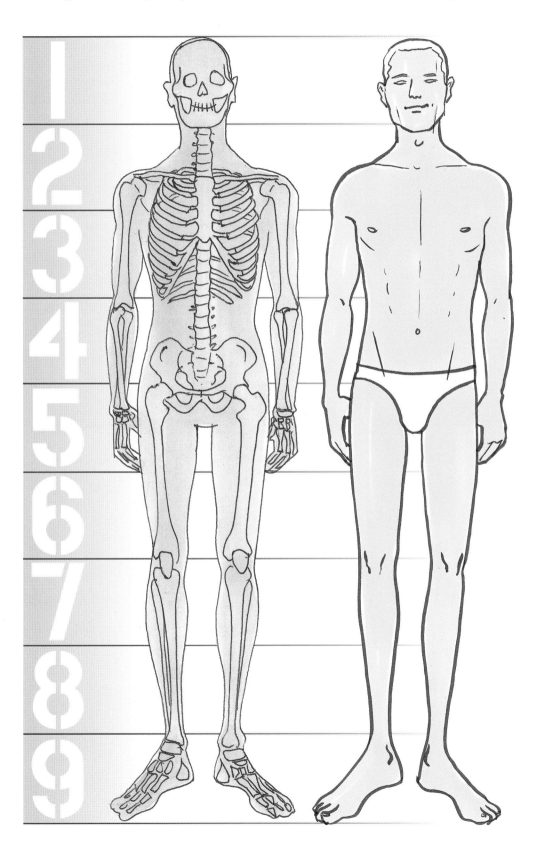

DIFFERENT AGES

Here we depict a whole family of figures, each with their own characteristics that must be taken into consideration when drawing in order to depict proportions accurately.

The fact that children have very different growth rates makes it difficult to create a definitive proportion template for each age group. As any parent knows, the size of garments for a specific age range can vary enormously from brand to brand. If you ever have to design or draw for a childrenswear company, they should supply their own size charts. There are, however, some general guidelines:

- A baby's head makes up about one-quarter of the total body length. By the age of one, the head is about two-thirds the size it will be when fully grown, so most of the growth thereafter will be seen in the body and limbs. Babies have short, almost invisible (from an artist's perspective) necks and large, round torsos. Their small, chubby limbs are bent rather than straight.
- Toddlers usually have a body that is about four and a half heads high. The shoulders are about the same width as the head height, and they have quite cylindrical bodies, sometimes with very round tummies. Poses should be fairly static for a toddler, since they are just learning to stand and walk, so the feet are firmly planted on the ground.
- Small children are about five heads tall. Since these lively little people rarely keep still, they can be depicted in more active poses.
- Bigger children range in height from six to six and a half heads, although by this age boys and girls can have very different heights. They still have cylindrical torsos and a very straight up-and-down silhouette, although older girls, from about the age of nine or ten, may start to have a slight indentation at the waistline, which is higher than a boy's. Older boys have longer torsos, slimmer hips, and slightly wider shoulders than girls.
- By the teenage years (sometimes called Junior in stores), children's height can be seven or eight heads. As hormonal changes take place, male and female forms become more pronounced, and the proportions of the teenage body are very different from a younger child's. Boys have

lower, slimmer hips and much longer torsos, which makes the arms and legs appear shorter. The differences are also apparent in head sizes, with girls having smaller heads and more petite facial features, which in boys tend to become more angular. As the body mass increases with age, the difference in muscularity between the genders becomes much more apparent.

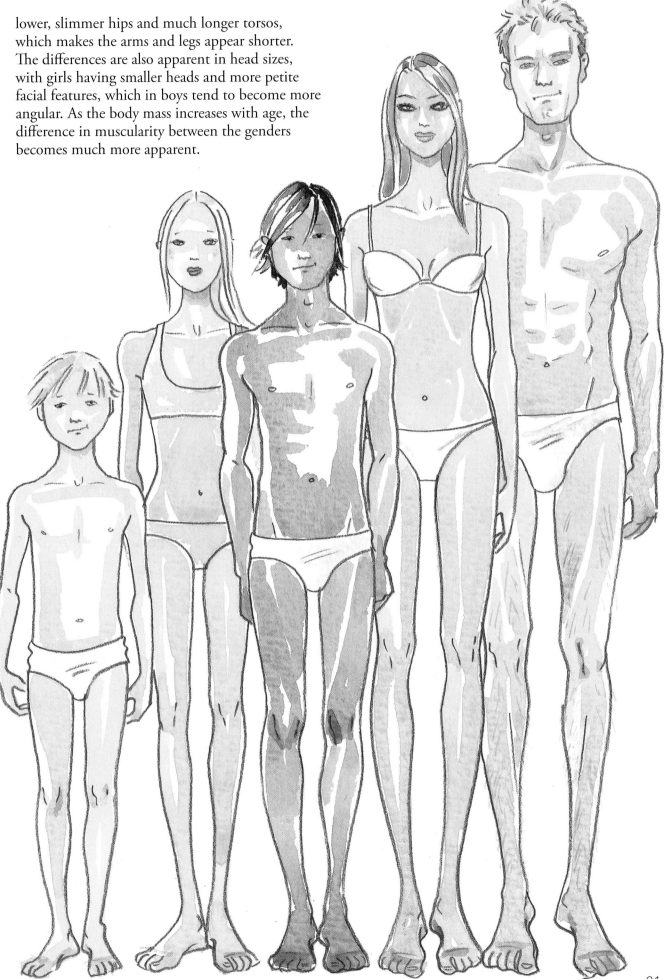

CREATING A TEMPLATE

STANDARD STRAIGHT-ON FRONT AND BACK VIEWS: WOMEN

Here we see how to draft a simple straight-on pose, viewed from the back and the front. You can see how the construction lines can be helpful when establishing the garment's design lines and proportions. Most designs need to be shown from the front and the back in order to fully explain the design.

The template also enables you to vary the position of the arms and legs. This is important because you may need to illustrate a detail such as the drape of a skirt or the volume of a sleeve, and altering the pose of the figure will allow you to accurately portray these design features.

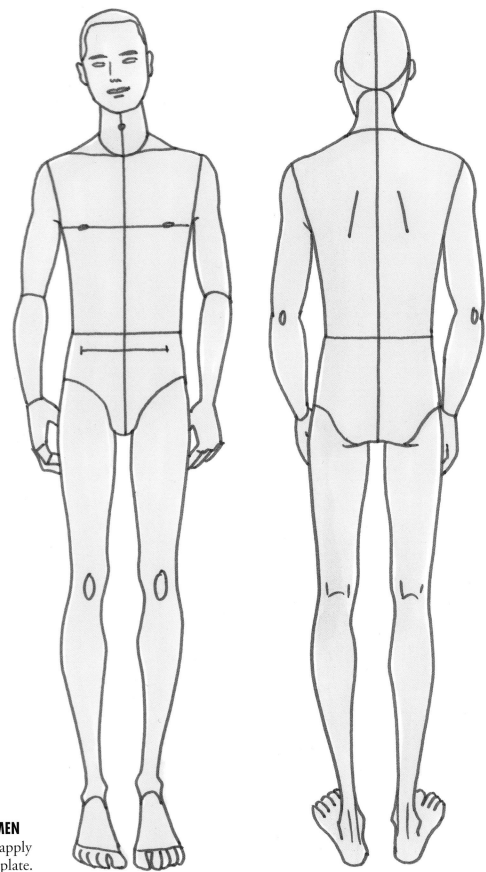

STANDARD STRAIGHT-ON FRONT AND BACK VIEWS: MEN
The same basic guidelines apply when drafting a man's template.

DRAWING HEADS

Having refined the pose of your figure, you can now transform it into a model with an image and identity. Facial expressions are key to creating an attitude or mood, and hair and makeup are strong indicators of period.

Collect pages from magazines for ideas and inspiration. Most heads are roughly egg shaped,

and the length of the face is generally the same as that of the hand, which is a useful guide when establishing proportions. Practice drawing a simple, expressionless face to start with, then as your confidence and style develop, you can begin to experiment with facial features and expressions to lend the model character.

DRAWING A FEMALE HEAD

1. *Draw an egg shape and two lines to mark a neck. Draw a vertical center line through the oval. This midline will be used to mark the position of the features. Remember that if the head tilts to one side, the line will, too.*

2. *Draw a horizontal line halfway down the head.*

3. *Draw in almond-shaped eyes on the horizontal midline, placing them about an eye's-width apart.*

4. *Mark the positions of the nose and mouth by dividing the lower half of the face into thirds.*

5. *To mark the width of the nose and mouth, draw downward vertical lines from the inner edge of the eye to give the width of the nose and the inner edge of the iris to show the width of the mouth. You can also roughly check the width of the neck by drawing lines vertically down from the outer edge of the eyes. The top of the ears should roughly align with the eyebrows and the bottom with the base of the nose.*

6. *Try adding some hairstyles. Remember, drawing hair does not involve showing every hair on the head—that's not what you see when you look at someone. It's the overall shape, color, and maybe a sense of movement that make an impression, and this overall look is what you should try to produce. The hairstyle you want to draw*

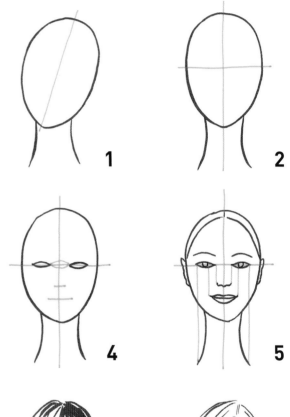
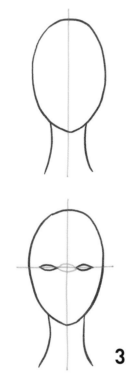

will affect your choice of medium. For fashion designers, the hair is secondary to the clothes, and they aim merely to give a quick impression of a style that works with the look. A few deft strokes with a brush pen can often be very

effective, and with a little practice, a smudge of oil pastel can produce a wonderful Pre-Raphaelite mane or a frizzy bob. Rough scribbles rarely work and tend to look messy rather than chic. Have fun experimenting.

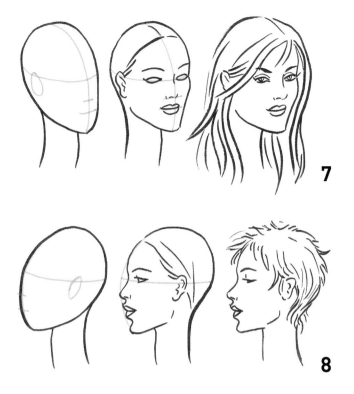

7. *The same principles for drawing a head front-on apply when showing a three-quarter view.*

8. *The same applies to a profile view.*

9. *Here we can see that the hand is roughly the same length as the face, from the hairline to the chin.*

7

8

9

DRAWING A MALE HEAD

Men's heads are frequently proportionally a little larger than women's, and following this guideline certainly helps to make a fashion drawing work better. Begin with a very basic shape. Here, the egg shape is somewhat squared off, and the squarer chin and jawline gives the face a masculine look. The neck will also be a little thicker than a woman's. Again, when adding hair you're drawing an impression of shape and color, not every strand. A broad stroke with a marker pen or a few waves drawn with a brush pen should suffice. Practice drawing people you know and using tear sheets from magazines as additional references for styles.

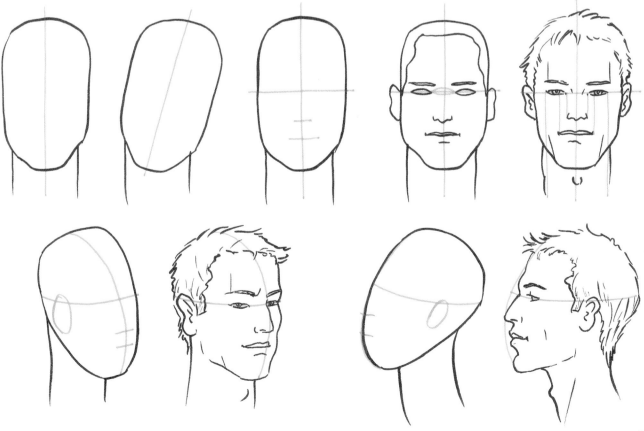

DRAWING HANDS AND FEET

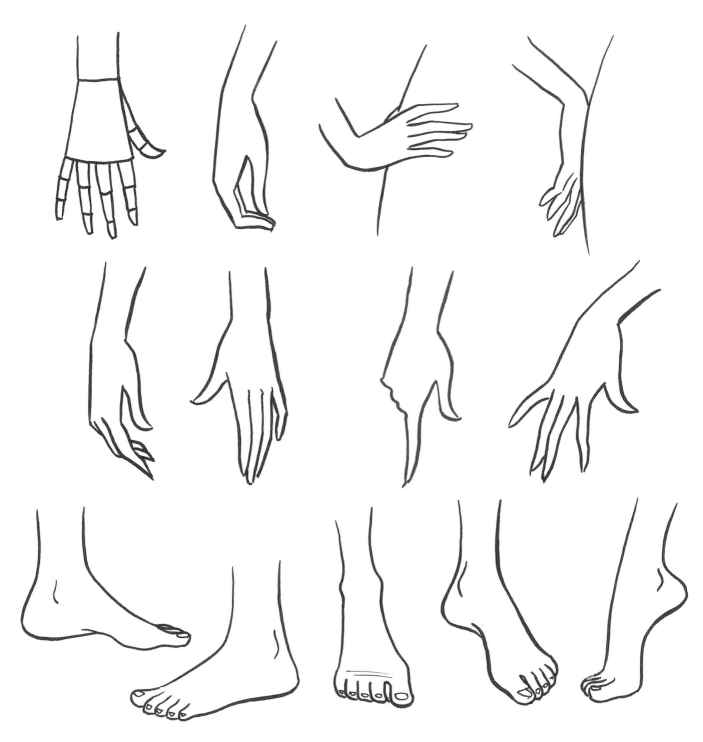

The hands and feet are often the body parts many people struggle to draw, and countless half-decent illustrations have been spoiled by the presence of claws or mittens for hands, blobs for feet, or tapering-out legs and no feet whatsoever.

Remembering the guideline that the length of the hand should match the length of the face will help you to get the right scale and proportion. Another

useful rule is that the distance from the wrist to the beginning of the fingers is approximately the same as the length of the fingers themselves. The trick is generally to keep it simple, with minimal details, and to break down the construction into basic shapes.

The illustrations above show a female hand and foot in various positions. Try copying the drawings, then try drawing your own hands and feet.

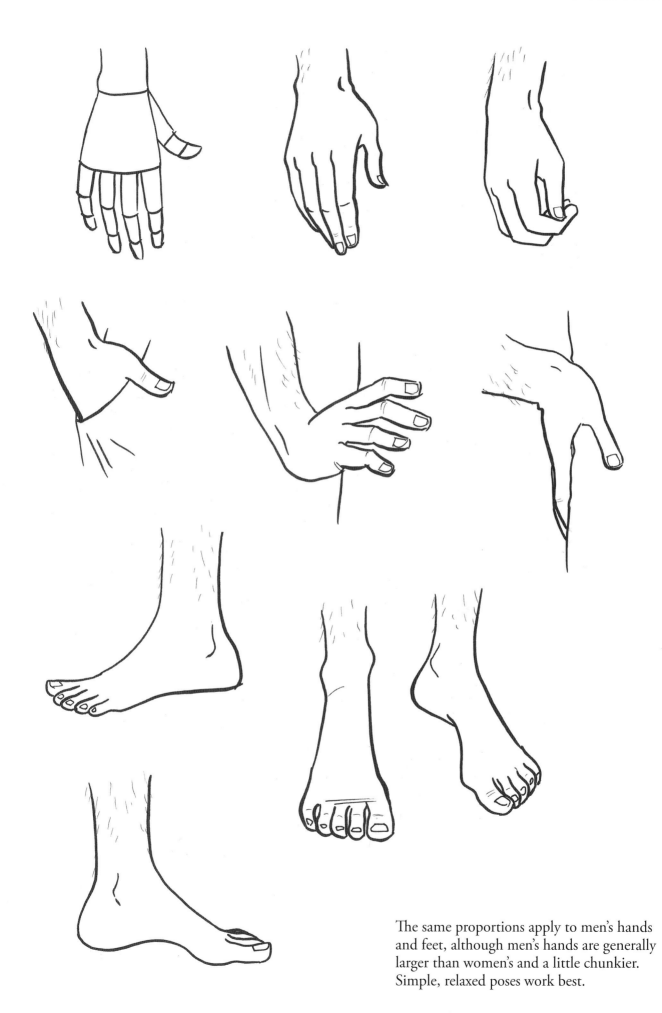

The same proportions apply to men's hands and feet, although men's hands are generally larger than women's and a little chunkier. Simple, relaxed poses work best.

CHAPTER 3

KEEPING AND USING A SKETCHBOOK

We have already touched upon the different types of sketchbooks available in stores in Chapter 1, but there is nothing to stop you from making a sketchbook yourself from an interesting collection of papers—or even from finding a vintage book and using that as a starting point. If the book contains images and text that are somehow related to your project then retain them; otherwise, you can stick new paper over pages or white out existing material with interior wall paint. If you choose to buy a new sketchbook, then you should make it your own, especially if it has a company logo on the front. Cover it with interesting paper that works for your project, or photocopy one of your own drawings and paste that onto the jacket.

It may be appropriate to have a separate sketchbook for a particular project or assignment, which will allow you a focused space for the development of your designs. But it is also a good idea to have what we might call a "general sketchbook" or "ideas book," in which you regularly jot notes and make quick sketches recording a thought, idea, or observation. Gather all kinds of information in the form of samples of color, postcards, images, pieces of packaging and wrapping paper, smudges of paint, snips of fabric, corners torn from magazines, press cuttings and magazine tears, addresses and information about exhibitions, and fashion blogs—anything that reminds, records, and inspires your creativity. However, whatever else goes in your sketchbook, remember that the clue is in the name—you should sketch in it!

When using a sketchbook you should not necessarily consider a possible future reader—it should be the place where you record, create, formulate, and document the development of ideas as well as solve problems, either in written or drawn form. However, if you know that a teacher or tutor is likely to want to see the sketchbook then it is worth making sure that everything is clear and attractively presented. Bearing an audience in mind may also help you during the development stages, enabling you to clarify thoughts and unify a concept by being prepared for reactions and questions.

Finally, a real sketchbook should never be put together at the end of an assignment or project; it should be a series of ideas that leads to a conclusion in the final designs and ideas, like the logbook of a creative journey or voyage of discovery.

Artwork by Sarah Cunningham

SKETCHBOOK INSPIRATION

Here we can see examples of how, during the early stages of a project, ephemera and "found images," such as postcards of paintings, magazine tear sheets, or photographs, can be used to inspire and spark ideas in a sketchbook. Examples shown here are by students from the University of Brighton, in the UK.

LEFT & BELOW: *This piece by Bryony Cooke builds a charming theme around the story of* I Capture The Castle *by Dodie Smith. It explores a nostalgic, domestic, 1950s "make-do" look with fresh colors, simple gingham-type fabrics, and a quirky little bird motif.*

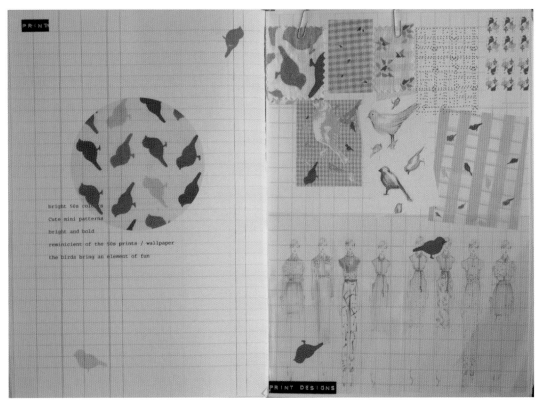

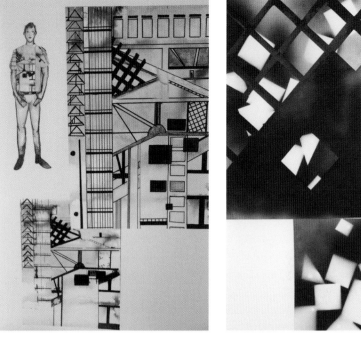

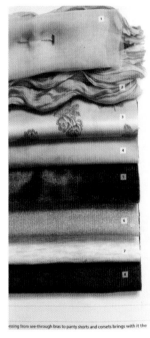

essing from see-through bras to panty shorts and corsets brings with it the

LEFT: *The designer Robert Atkins' photographs of architecture and architectural details reveal an interest in patterns and grid structures that lead to a series of ideas for prints and patterned menswear in a university CAD (Computer Aided Design) project.*

LEFT: *In this sketchbook, Sarah Cunningham uses a found image of blossoms to inspire a color palette that has been expressed using colored yarns and embroidery threads. The roughly but thoughtfully torn packing paper is suggestive of soft petal edges and makes a good neutral background for the color combinations. Embroidery threads are widely available in a range of tones and make a good choice of medium for accurately depicting colors.*

RIGHT: *This example from a sketchbook (also by a student from the University of Brighton) again uses a simple found image. Sorbets in glasses inspire a fresh, summery color palette. Subtle irregularities in the shape and size of the colored yarn windings lend spontaneity and a handmade quality to the piece.*

RESEARCH AND DESIGN

Sketchbooks are inseparable from research and design. If your sketchbook is a logbook of your journey, then research is what you observe, discover, and find inspiring on that journey, and design is how you filter, generate, and connect ideas and thoughts and focus them into some kind of conclusion—an end concept or product. Research is what stimulates ideas. There is also practical research, which might be looking into techniques, processes, fabrics, and materials, and this informs and makes those ideas happen. Design development is essentially the aesthetic and practical process of cycling through many permutations of one idea—which will often lead you to more ideas—and by evaluating, refining, and critically assessing those themes, eventually you arrive at a finished design.

Although found material, as already discussed, is very important for stimulating ideas, the work that appears in a sketchbook should be mostly primary research, that is to say, things you have drawn and researched firsthand: photographs you have taken, experiments and discoveries made by going, doing, seeing, and experiencing things for yourself. The more personal your research, the more individual your creative outcomes will be. Allow yourself to be inspired by almost anything, from a vacation or museum trip to something more obscure and esoteric, and build upon that first spark of an idea, developing a thread that leads from initially random inclusions in your sketchbook to a final conclusion.

If your starting point is, for instance, Ancient Egypt, you should eschew obvious mainstream sources of information, such as the masses of books on the subject, and instead find out whether a collection is being exhibited in a museum or historical house and if so, go there yourself to draw and photograph (where possible) inspiring artifacts. You might watch some old movies, too, and find out about other fashion trends that have been influenced by the same theme over the years, such as the passion for Egyptian styles in France and Regency Britain following Napoleon's campaigns in Egypt and Syria in the late 1700s. Thus, it is easy to see how making connections and imaginative leaps and layering influences can help you develop an idea and lend it a personal slant; it's a little bit like following a basic recipe and adding some alternative ingredients to give it a twist. Research is always exciting—expect the unexpected.

Inclusions in your sketchbook research may be drawings, images, or notes or other information about color, shapes, and pattern, form, texture, fabrics and materials, construction, detail, atmosphere, scale, history, or background. You should cross reference or juxtapose images or details within images. The relevance of images and the connections between one image or idea and another should become apparent; as you progress, your creative thought process should be evident and purposeful, especially to you.

DUSTER COAT PROJECT by Yvonne Deacon

1. *This project takes inspiration from a favorite vintage find—a linen duster coat or warehouseman's coat from the 1930s. Other found images were combined to set a mood, including an old grocery bill and a black and white photograph of a grocery store from the early twentieth century, with the owner proudly standing in front of his wares. A painting by Cézanne showing a card player wearing a similar coat was also included, together with nostalgic old photographs of a small boy in interesting clothes and a girl on a bike in a print dress. A few swatches of coarse linen and a piece of red thread were later turned into the red stitching feature that appears on the final design.*

2. *A flat or semidiagrammatical sketch was made of the coat, revealing its lovely details and proportions. The utility aspect was considered important, and this was enhanced by the inclusion of scraps of coarse, hardwearing linen that demonstrated its surface finish, texture, and color after many washes. A charming pencil and crayon sketch of a thrush with its chest puffed up and wings akimbo give rise to ideas about air and volume, and its subtle plumage, along with vintage-look floral fabrics inspired by the bicycling girl, led to the development of the color story. Loose sketches record and develop initial ideas and silhouettes, and these combine to build the mood.*

1

2

3

4

3. *The theme and atmosphere are clarified in a "mood board" showing other researched, drawn, and found images. Photographs of the actual coat show the thought progression and are supported by a painted and collaged color palette.*

4. *"Design development sheets" show the development of the design ideas. The silhouette is drawn and redrawn, with proportions and details being exaggerated and explored repeatedly*

5. *Further series of design developments refine the possibilities for the coat, which is to be the key item in this capsule collection. The functional appeal of its pockets and details are enhanced with bold stitching.*

6. *The notion of layering—which goes back to the source of the idea in terms of overalls, aprons, protection, and volume—is explored in this series of developments.*

5

6

7

8a

8b

7. *The ideas are further developed to include a more literal interpretation of the thrush, with ideas for embroidered wings and speckled and spotted fabrics.*

8. *The project finishes with a series of more precise design drawings showing the refined ideas and details, and these are clear enough to be used for starting to make up the designs. The last illustration (8c) consists of a precise drawing on tracing paper layered over standard paper on which fabric color and pattern have been rendered in a loose, interpretive way. This technique complements the layered aspect of the garment's design.*

8c

CHAPTER 4

DRAWING FABRIC

Once you have mastered the basics of figure drawing and creating effective poses, the next stage is learning how to draw the clothes. This is a little like making them, so this section reveals how to draw fabric as part of that process. It is a good idea to develop an understanding of the range of fabrics available, since this will enable you to realize how integral cloth is to the character and identity of garments. How this knowledge informs your designs is part of the next step; it is not about replicating a piece of fabric on paper (although that is good practice), it's more about developing your own visual shorthand.

Wherever it is possible, try to have samples of the fabrics in front of you or at least some magazine tear sheets of similar fabrics so you know what you are trying to represent. Then try out a range of different mediums until you achieve something you are happy with. Always allow yourself time to experiment and to create the actual artwork, taking into account drying times for mediums such as paint and glue. As with most creative work, a little planning in advance will help you to achieve the best results.

BASIC TECHNIQUES FOR RENDERING FABRIC

Choosing a suitable type of paper is the first stage. Very smooth paper is perfect for depicting satin or shiny fabrics, while watercolor paper may be better for showing rustic tweed or a soft mélange knit. These papers can then be collaged into your drawings. Similarly, you can scan or photocopy the actual fabrics, reduce the scale, and stick them onto the page as required.

Having drawn an outline of the design, you can lay down a base color using a marker pen, paint, or oil pastel and then work more detail in with crayon, felt-tip pens, ink, gel pens, oil, or all of the above! You could also start by using a "resist" for part of the detail, which involves blocking out an area with wax crayon or a candle or with professional watercolor masking fluid. You then apply a base color over the top, and the detail will remain uncolored. If you are using masking fluid, remove it once the base paint is dry. You can then add more detail using another medium. This method can work particularly well for damask and lace-type fabrics with shadow or sheen effects, or for those materials with a bolder positive/negative aspect.

Fabrics from The Cloth Shop

WHITE FABRIC

Drawing white fabrics might seem like an easy option, but varying their characteristics brings its own set of challenges that need to be surmounted creatively. In these examples, surface luster and texture are cleverly suggested using bold strokes and a sensitive choice of mediums that reflect the type of material being depicted.

Voile is a type of fine, sheer fabric. Traditionally, it was always expensive as it was technically more challenging to create fine fabrics, and so it was used for special-occasion garments, such as party or wedding dresses, fine shirts, and so on. Other sheer fabrics include chiffon, georgette, and tulle. These days, thanks to mechanization and man-made fibers, such sheer fabrics have become more affordable and available and are no longer associated exclusively with occasion wear.

Traditionally, lurex and lamé fabrics have metallic threads woven into them, but modern versions of these materials often also incorporate synthetic fibers, and metallic effects are created using foiling and printing techniques.

In the illustration below, good-quality brown wrapping paper was used as drawing paper, afterward drafting the design the outline was inked in. Chalk pencil was lightly applied to the dress, and further shading was added using marker pen and pencil crayon.

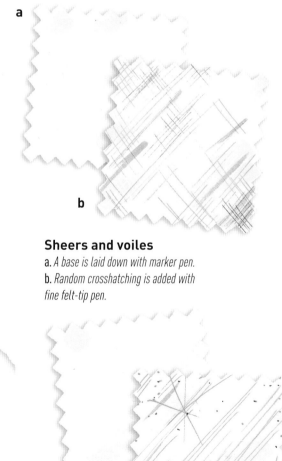

a

b

Sheers and voiles
a. *A base is laid down with marker pen.*
b. *Random crosshatching is added with fine felt-tip pen.*

a

b

Lurex and lamé
a. *A base is laid down with marker pen.*
b. *Random dots and lines and sparkly lines/stars are added using fine felt-tip pen.*

Broderie anglaise, sometimes known as "Swiss embroidery," is traditionally a fine white cotton fabric with a pattern of eyelets hand-embroidered onto it, usually in white thread, although European variants often used colored embroidery threads. Today, there are many variations on this type of fabric, and it is almost always machine-made.

Crochet is a handmade fabric that, unlike knitting, cannot be created by machine even to produce the most simple stitches and designs. Crochet is used to create pretty openwork patterns for decorative trims and finishes and sometimes to produce clever bas-relief and 3D effects.

Lace, with some variants known as "thread-lace," covers a broad family of openwork fabrics, including net. The fabric often has strong cultural roots, and particular regions and countries are famous for the different techniques used and the complexity and design of the finished products. While lace was traditionally handmade, machine-made lace began to appear at the height of the Industrial Revolution, and mechanized lace production is still developing today.

Guipure lace, despite its name, is a type of embroidery rather than lace, and so it is sometimes known by its proper name "guipure lace embroidery." It is created by applying a pattern of thread embroidery to a ground fabric, which is then removed by chemical or other means to leave an openwork lace.

In this example of a 1960s-inspired cocktail shift dress, guipure lace is suggested by using a little stamp to print a pattern on the illustration, using irregular pressure to avoid a flat finish.

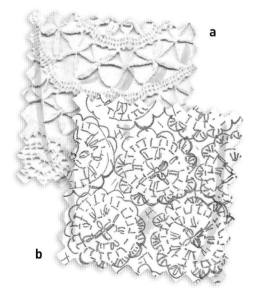

Broderie anglaise
a. *A base is laid down with marker pen.*
b. *Felt-tip pen is used for the eyelets.*

Crochet
a. *Real crochet is scanned into a computer and then printed.*
b. *Pale gray fine felt-tip pen is used to draw the fabric.*

Lace
A craft stamp is used to create a light print with black ink fading to gray, and details are added with fine felt-tip pen.

LUXURY FABRICS

This satin evening dress was drawn on watercolor paper in pencil outline before loose, bold strokes of watercolor were added.

Satin is a smooth, generally lustrous fabric with a close, warp-faced woven surface that catches and reflects the light. Traditionally made from silk, many versions made from synthetic fabrics are also available today. Sateen is similar to satin but is a weft-faced fabric.

Velvet is fabric woven with a pile surface. This is created during the manufacturing process by lifting the warp over wires to make loops and then cutting them as the wires are withdrawn. Similar fabrics are plush and velour. Terry, sometimes known as "terry cloth" is created in a similar way, but the loops are not cut. There are knitted versions of all of these types of pile fabrics, which have the advantage of the degree of stretch associated with most knitted fabrics.

Sequins are sometimes known by their French name, *paillettes*. Traditionally, they are small reflective metallic disks sewn onto fabrics, although modern versions come in all kinds of finishes, including matte, transparent, printed, and hologram. They are available in a variety of sizes and shapes.

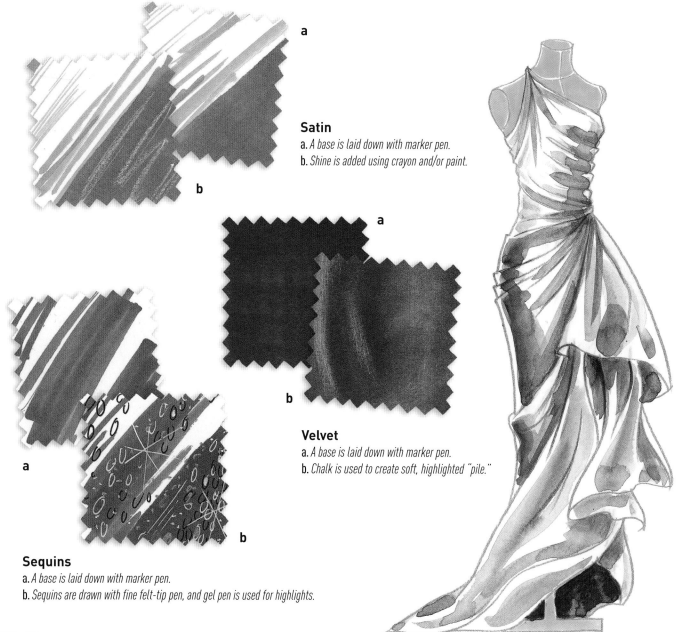

Satin
a. *A base is laid down with marker pen.*
b. *Shine is added using crayon and/or paint.*

Velvet
a. *A base is laid down with marker pen.*
b. *Chalk is used to create soft, highlighted "pile."*

Sequins
a. *A base is laid down with marker pen.*
b. *Sequins are drawn with fine felt-tip pen, and gel pen is used for highlights.*

ANIMAL PATTERNS, FUR, AND BROCADE

The loose category of "animal patterns" covers a range of designs, inspired originally by the markings and textures found on real animal coats. Leopard-skin, cheetah-skin, and snakeskin are perennial favorites in the fashion world. New digital printing techniques have resulted in ever-increasing possibilities with regard to the scale of the pattern and repeat. Such has been the popularity of animal prints in recent years that designers are now creating fantasy hybrid patterns that incorporate elements from birds' plumage, patterns found on moths and butterflies, and other variants from the natural world.

Fur, traditionally the skins and coats of dead animals, is used to create very warm garments.

The rarity and/or attractiveness of certain animals once elevated these fabrics to luxury status, but the wearing of real fur is now highly controversial, particularly since modern manufacturing can reproduce convincing synthetic versions.

Brocade is a woven fabric related to satin in terms of the technique used to make it. Patterns are usually created by contrasting areas of raised or floated warp threads against a more simply structured ground. Some variants contrast warp threads against weft threads in a similar way.

This eye-catching coat was drawn with a pencil outline on watercolor paper. Masking fluid was used to create a pattern, and watercolor paint was applied.

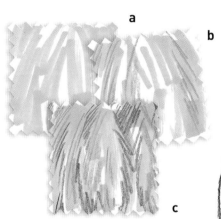

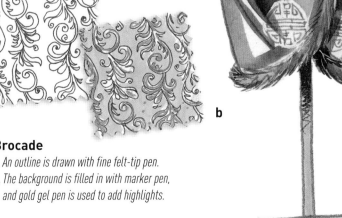

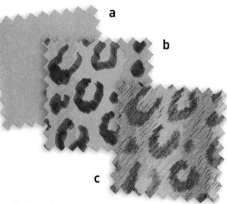

Fur
a. *A base is laid down with marker pen.*
b. *Shaggy texture is added with pencil crayon.*
c. *The final touches are applied with pencil crayon and gel pens.*

Animal patterns
a. *A base is laid down with marker pen.*
b. *A pattern is applied with felt-tip pen.*
c. *Alternatively, a pattern can be added with pencil crayon to give a softer-looking option.*

Digital animal prints
Animal-print fabric is scanned into a computer and then printed.

Brocade
a. *An outline is drawn with fine felt-tip pen.*
b. *The background is filled in with marker pen, and gold gel pen is used to add highlights.*

Brocade
A design is drawn in wax resist (see page 39) first, then lightly brushed over with watercolor.

KNIT

Knitting is an ancient method of hand-making fabric and garments that has many cultural roots worldwide, from northern Scotland to Peru and many other countries besides. Most of the knitted patterns, such as Fair Isle, Aran, or cable, that we are familiar with today have origins going back several centuries. Trade and cultural migration has led to many stylistic similarities, resulting in patterns being grouped under a single name, such as "Nordic," which includes the traditional patterns of Scandinavia, Northern Europe, and the Baltic. Since the invention of the earliest knitting machines in the late sixteenth century for the stocking trade, manufacturers have developed and refined the processes, and today machines are able to produce incredibly sophisticated and intricate knitted fabrics and garments. Despite this, perhaps surprisingly, many modern garments are still hand-knitted.

In this men's outfit, the soft, warm texture of the Nordic-look sweater is suggested by the subtle coloring, which is applied using marker pens and a little soft pencil crayon for the shadows and the chunky rib trims. The skinny jeans are first rendered with a base of deep blue marker pen, then shadows and highlights are applied with darker and lighter crayons. Fine diagonal pencil crayon marks help to suggest the twill weave of denim.

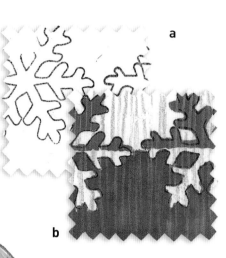

Nordic
a. *A craft stamp is used to apply a pattern.*
b. *Marker pen is used to apply color, then texture is added with a pencil crayon.*

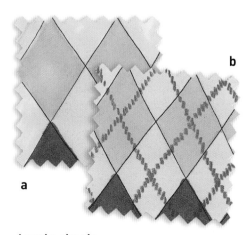

Argyle check
a. *After drafting a basic pattern in pencil, the diamond shapes are colored with marker pen.*
b. *Pencil crayon is used to draw in the colored rakes.*

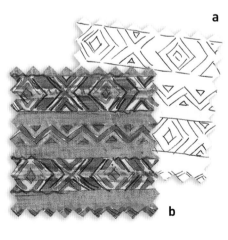

Fair Isle
a. *A pattern is drafted first in pencil, then defined with fine felt-tip pen.*
b. *Marker pens and pencil crayons are used to add texture and depth of color.*

The young woman's outfit combines a soft, semisheer fluted skirt—suggested by using delicate brush pen strokes and light crayoning—and a chunky cable-patterned sweater and a simple knitted scarf, both of which are rendered using controlled and restrained pencil crayon marks.

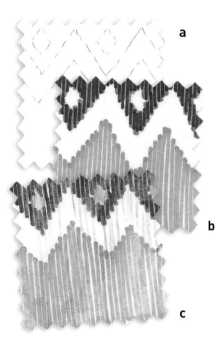

Nordic

a. *A pattern is first drafted in pencil.*
b. *Marker pen adds delicate color, and the pencil marks are erased.*
c. *Texture and depth of color are rendered using pencil crayon.*

Textured stitches

a. *A pattern is mapped out in pencil, if possible using a real stitch reference for accuracy and clarity.*
b. *The pattern is defined with marker pen, then the pencil is erased. Texture and depth of color are applied with pencil crayon.*

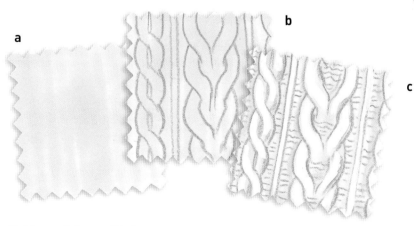

Cable and Aran stitches

a. *A base color is applied with marker pen.*
b. *A pattern is carefully mapped out in pencil crayon.*
c. *Shading and definition are applied with toning pencil crayons.*

HARDWEARING FABRIC

Leather
Marker pen is used to create variations of tone.

Distressed leather
An oil pastel rubbing on a rough surface creates a distressed effect.

Leather has two principal qualities that fashion perpetually exploits and celebrates: The first is luxury—the depth of color, supple feel of the fabric, and the craftsmanship associated with handling this relatively difficult material; the second is (perhaps conversely) its tough rebel image, which has its origins in the youth movements of the late 1950s, 60s and 70s, and which is somehow enhanced by signs of wear and tear.

Canvas and denim are tough, relatively coarse-grain fabrics, which have their origins in utility wear. One of the most-loved qualities of denim is the way in which it fades and wears, a quality we associate with individuality and a certain rebel spirit, although much of the denim we buy today is already faded.

Twill is a type of textile weave that repeats on three or more ends or "picks," which produces the diagonal grain that is characteristic of twill fabric.

For this cool biker girl look, the jeans are again rendered with a base of deep blue marker pen with shadows and highlights applied with darker and lighter crayons. Fine diagonal pencil crayon marks suggest the twill weave of denim, and there are pronounced faded effects as well as delicately drawn and shaded rips and holes. By only partially coloring the jacket, the effect of shine and highlights on softly worn leather is created. Marker pen and a little correction fluid are used to finish a sparkly top.

Canvas
a. *A base is applied with marker pen.*
b. *An oil pastel rubbing creates texture.*

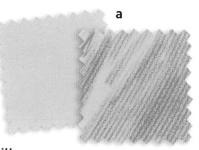

Twill
a. *A base is applied with marker pen.*
b. *A rubbing using marker pen produces a textured finish.*

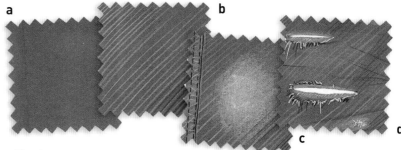

Denim
a. *A base is applied with marker pen.*
b. *Diagonal twill lines are added with pencil crayon.*
c. *Stitching is rendered with black felt-tip pen and worn areas with pastel crayon.*
d. *Pastel crayon and white gel pen are used to add rips.*

The idea of camouflage was first understood by hunters, who took their inspiration from the animals they pursued and their habitats. Although the notion was taken up by the military in the eighteenth century, it did not really develop into the wide range of specialist fabric patterns we know and recognize today until World Wars I and II.

Felt is a dense, textured fabric, the surface of which is compacted and flattened during the manufacturing process to make it very hardwearing.

Corduroy is a woven fabric similar to velvet in its construction, with a cut weft pile. The vertical lines of the pile, running parallel to the warp, are known as "wales," the same as the vertical lines of rib structures in knitting.

This figure's dark reefer jacket or peacoat could have been flat and lifeless, but deliberately leaving exposed white ground and further highlighting the seams and structure in white pen gave it clarity and definition. The twisted and loosely wrapped, striped scarf has been accurately represented. A base has been applied with marker pen, and bold china marker lines are used to create the look of soft chunky corduroy pants.

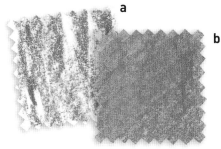

Camouflage
a. *A base is applied with marker pen.*
b. *A pattern is added with another shade of marker pen.*
c. *More overlapping marker pen shapes are layered to create the desired effect.*

Felt
a. *A base is applied with oil pastel.*
b. *A second tone in oil pastel is blended with white spirit, then another rough layer of oil pastel is added on top.*

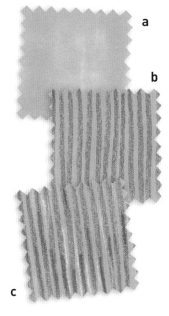

Needle and wide-wale corduroy
a. *A base color is applied with marker pen.*
b. *Vertical strokes in oil pastel indicate the texture.*
c. *White pencil crayon is used to add highlights.*

Corduroy—alternative
A base color is applied with marker pen, then a rubbing on a ribbed surface is made using oil pastel.

MENSWEAR FABRIC

Tweed, originally a heavyweight woolen fabric used for outerwear, was traditionally woven in southern Scotland. The name is taken from the Tweed River, the water of which was used to wash and finish the fabric. Today, the term *tweed* applies to a wide range of look-alike fabrics. One of its principal attractions is the mix of pleasing colors that are made possible by the dying and weaving techniques used. Donegal in Ireland lends its name to a speckled, napped, tweed-type fabric that was unique to the area.

The quality of the drawing below and the successful rendering of the fabrics have been greatly helped by the choice of the beautifully grainy Ingres paper. The tweed jacket is created with a marker pen base to which oil pastel shadowing and flecks of color using soft crayon have been added. The pinstripe fabric of the pants is rendered with a rough background of marker pen to which vertical lines have been applied using white pen, all toning with the hues of the jacket and tie in a pleasing way.

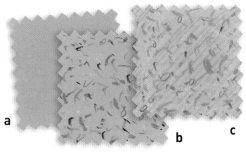

Donegal tweed
a. *A base is applied with marker pen.*
b. *Random dots are added with pencil crayon and pastel.*
c. *The impression of neps (small balls of fiber on the surface of a fabric) and texture is created with pencil crayon.*

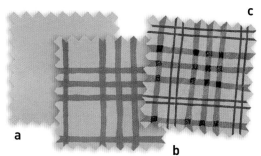

Heritage plaid
a. *A base is applied with marker pen.*
b. *Check lines are added with marker pen.*
c. *Pencil crayon is used for overlaid check lines.*

Shepherd's check
(and gingham-type structured fabrics)
a. *With a penciled grid as a guide, diagonal lines are used to create two vertical columns in felt-tip pen.*
b. *Horizontal columns of diagonal lines are added to create a check.*
c. *The crossover points of the columns are emphasized by coloring in these areas more solidly.*
d. *The check size can be varied by changing the width of the columns and their distance apart.*

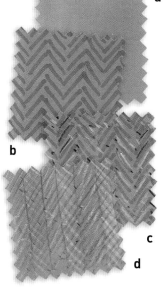

Herringbone tweed
a. *A base is applied with marker pen.*
b. *The basic herringbone structure is added with marker pen.*
c. *Pencil crayon is used to add highlights and tweed effects.*
d. *An alternative technique is to use pencil crayon to mark the pattern onto the marker pen base (see "Soft muted herringbone" on facing page).*

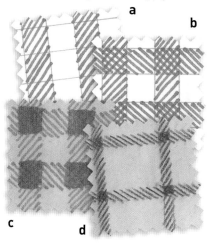

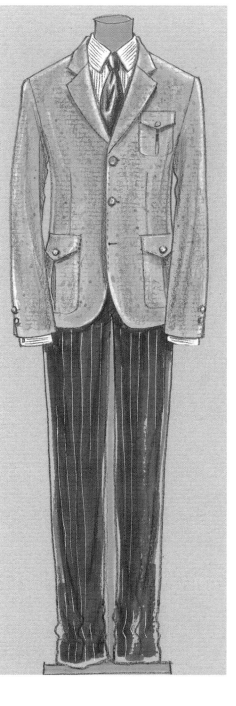

e term *herringbone* describes a traditional woven
tern created using a twill (diagonal) weave that
eversed after several courses to produce stripes
embling herringbones.

Shepherd's check is created in contrasting colors
grouping four, six, or eight threads of two colors
d using a twill weave. The name probably
ginated from the plaids worn by shepherds in the
ls of the Scottish Borders. Houndstooth or
gstooth are variations of this weave. Many of the
nting estates of the British aristocracy developed
ir own characteristic check colors and patterns

that have become known collectively as estate tweeds
or often as heritage plaids.

Gingham is a plain weave cotton fabric in which
a square construction of dyed yarns is contrasted
against white or undyed yarns to form small checks.

On this page, deft lines of marker pen create the
ribbed roll-neck sweater. For the overcoat, marker
pen was used for the base, with the herringbone
pattern completed in fine felt-tip pen. White gel
pen was used for highlights and lowlights. The pants
were drawn with a base of marker pen, then crayon
was used for the shadows and highlights.

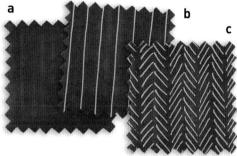

Pinstripe and fine herringbone

a. *A dark base is applied with marker pen.*
b. *The pin stripe is drawn with white gel pen.*
c. *The herringbone pattern is drawn with gel pen for a fine, crisp effect.*

Soft muted herringbone

This tweed version of the herringbone pattern is drawn using soft pencil crayon over a dark marker pen base.

Glen plaid

a. *A base is applied with marker pen.*
b. *Bands of vertical lines are added with fine felt-tip pen.*
c. *Bands of horizontal lines are similarly added using fine felt-tip pen, and pencil crayon over the top adds texture and depth.*

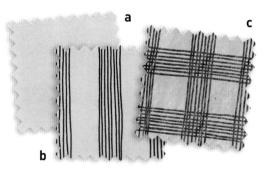

Houndstooth check *(sometimes called dogtooth)*

a. *Using a grid drawn in pencil, squares are marked out as shown with marker pen.*
b. *The grid is erased and diagonal lines are added to link the boxes vertically using fine felt-tip pen.*
c. *Lateral diagonal lines link the boxes horizontally.*

PRINTS

Printing is a way of creating pattern on fabric after it has been woven. Fabric has been printed by various cultures throughout the world for thousands of years. The invention of roller printing at the end of the eighteenth century revolutionized the process and made patterned fabrics affordable for almost everyone. Modern digital printing processes are again changing the industry, solving problems that have until now restricted the number of colors it is possible to print and the scale of repeated patterns.

Polka dots
a. A dark base is applied with marker pen.
b. Polka dots can be added using self-adhesive white dots.
c. Alternatively, polka dots can be drawn with designers' gouache.

Dolly florals
A floral pattern is drawn onto a dark base using calligraphy pen and ink.

Retro prints
a. A pattern is drawn with pencil, then black lines are added with ink.
b. Marker pen is used to fill in background color, and the pencil lines are erased.
c. A base is applied with marker pen.
d. Black brush pen is used to apply the pattern.
e. Pattern is drawn in with gray brush pen.
f. Marker pens are used to fill in color.

Collage
Any existing pattern, such as different fabrics, wrapping paper, craft paper, or origami paper, can be scanned and applied.

Cotton fabric is woven from cotton fiber, which forms in a boll (protective capsule) around the seeds of a species of plants of the genus *Gossypium* and is unraveled and treated to form the long strands that are used for making fabric. It is grown in many regions of the world, and the cotton fibers vary from country to country, with each having their own particular qualities and advantages. Egyptian cotton plants, for instance, produce very long fibers that are woven to create one of the finest cotton fabrics, which is used for making high-quality shirts and fine bed linen. Patterned cotton falls into two distinct categories—woven and printed. Woven patterns include variations of stripes and checks that are created by using contrasting colors of thread in the warp and weft. Printed patterns cover almost every other type of pattern possible.

This floral dress was drawn using a soft pencil outline on watercolor paper. Pattern and some light shadows were added in watercolor. Pencil crayon was used for shading and definition.

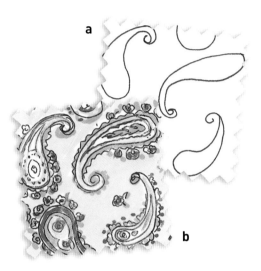

Scanned fabrics
Floral fabrics can be scanned and used as collage material.

Paisley
a. *The pattern is lightly drawn in pencil, then traced over with fine felt-tip pen and the pencil is erased.*
b. *Color is added with marker pen and pencil crayons.*

Chintz
a. *A pattern is drawn with fine pencil.*
b. *The main colors are added with watercolor; then, when it is fully dry, the pencil is erased, and definition and finer detail are applied on top with pencil crayon.*

CHAPTER 5

DRAWING GARMENTS AND OUTFITS

With a broader knowledge of fabrics—their qualities, characteristics, and behavior—and a better understanding and appreciation of garment details and construction, you can approach the challenge of fashion drawing with confidence. So it follows that the next essential step is to learn something about the construction of clothes, including details such as how a shirt collar works and sits around a neckline, how a jacket rever or lapel folds and rolls, and how shirt cuffs and plackets, pockets, epaulettes, gathers, pleats, and so on function. Similarly, you will draw a silhouette better if you understand how the outline is achieved—where the volume comes from and how it is suppressed, reduced, or controlled.

You can obtain much of this information simply by paying attention to clothes and studying them with a critical eye, either at home or in stores. Ask questions such as: What is happening here? How is that shape created? How does that neckline or fastening work? There is nothing to stop you from trying something on in a store (or asking a friend of the opposite gender to try it on for you), so you can better understand the subtleties and complexities of the construction. Take a closer look and turn the garment inside out, if necessary in the privacy of the changing room. Good drawing comes from good seeing. When it comes to designing, part of the function of drawing is about communicating how the garment is constructed and resolving any issues so that it can be realized successfully.

Remember, although you may be trying to draw an idea, something new out of your head, there is always something at hand to help you to understand how to draw that notion, be it a real garment with a similar feature or the reference material you have gathered in your sketchbook—your collection of found images, magazine tear sheets, museum and costume drawings, and so on. Even draping some fabric in similar fashion across a dress stand or yourself in front of a mirror can spark your imagination and help you to explain and communicate your ideas in your sketches. Keep trying out different variations until you hit on an illustration that works—ideas evolve as they are drawn, and different possibilities present themselves with each adaptation. Above all, have fun!

URBAN GIRL

1. *Trace a model from your template, amending limb positions as required.*

2. *Plot the silhouette of the outfit and the positioning of main details, such as the depth and angle of the neckline and collar. Use a light pencil mark that can be easily erased and altered. Still using pencil, lightly add the hairstyle, facial features, and accessories. Remember the clothes should be drawn slightly larger than the figure itself so they look realistic and not skin tight.*

3. *Once you are happy that everything looks right, ink in the outlines and strongest details with a medium-thick felt-tip pen or a brush pen. Erase the pencil marks.*

4. *Having completed the outline, you can add color using marker pens, watercolor—which produces a more fluid appearance and allows you to mix your own shades—or oil pastels, which give a softer, blurred look. Marker pens are ideal for adding skin tones at this stage. Best results are often achieved by not taking the color all the way to the edges of the outlines; completely colored-in drawings can seem very flat and lifeless. Using a marker pen in quick, light directional strokes also helps to enhance the appearance of the pleats in the skirt and gives the effect of movement.*

5. *Add fine fabric details such as texture and print with pencil crayons and wax crayons. Add a little shadowing to help enhance the layering effects and give a more 3D look to collars, pockets, and so on. You might want to emphasize topstitching or add shine at the edge of a button. Using white pencil crayon on medium to dark fabrics can help to add definition. Makeup has been added to the face and highlights to the hair.*

PARTY GIRL

1

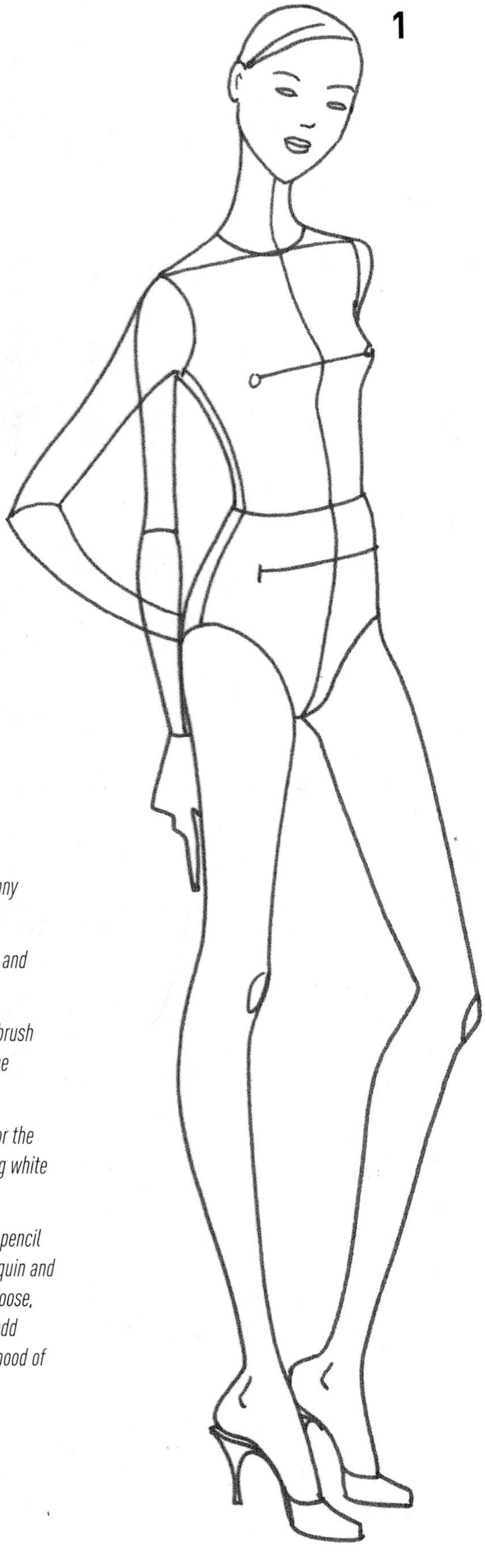

2

1. Choose your template and make any minor adjustments to the pose.

2. Map out and refine the silhouette and proportions in pencil.

3. Ink in the dress and figure using brush pen and fine felt-tip pen. Erase the pencil marks.

4. Use marker pens sparingly to color the dress, skin tones, and hair, leaving white paper showing for highlights.

5. Use soft pencil crayon and grainy pencil to add shading, then apply the sequin and sparkle details on the dress in a loose, free style. Use pencil crayons to add makeup and complete the party mood of the outfit.

URBAN GUY

1. *Choose your template and make any minor adjustments to the pose.*

2. *Draw the whole outfit in pencil, checking the proportions and making final decisions about details.*

3. *Once you are satisfied, use a brush pen and fine felt-tip pens to finalize the outlines, structure, and details. Note how small broken lines are used here to suggest the fleece/pile fabric of the hood lining.*

4. *Use light colored pencil strokes to indicate the relatively complex pattern of the jacquard Nordic-look sweater. Marker pens are best for blocking in base colors for the jeans and roll-neck sweater.*

5. *Continue adding delicate marks with fine felt-tip pen to build up the sweater's pattern, keeping the pattern loose and not too defined to indicate a soft, wool-like feel rather than a flat, printed look. Use a pencil crayon to add soft shading and highlights to the sweater and jeans. Apply additional diagonal strokes of pencil crayon to the jeans to depict a grainy denim look.*

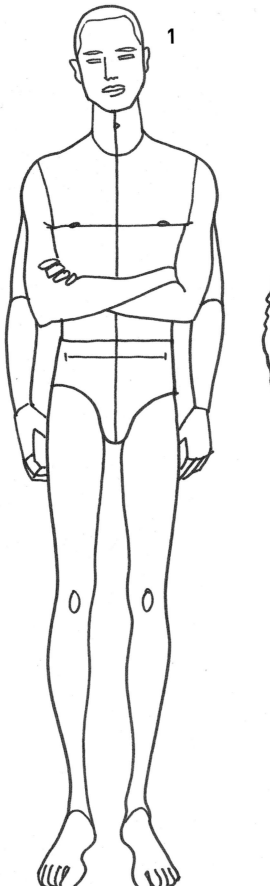

1

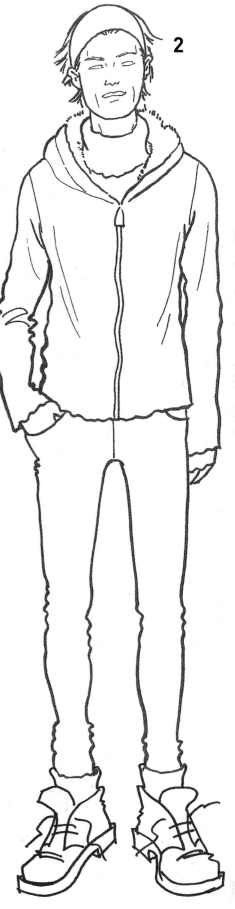

2

PARTY GUY

1. *Choose your template and make any minor adjustments to the pose.*

2. *Using pencil, sketch the basic fit, proportions, and details of the garments and accessories.*

3. *Use brush pen and fine felt-tip pen to ink in the outlines and details, then erase the pencil marks.*

4. *Use marker pens to add color. Black fabric is always hard to draw, and although marker pens give a good density of color, you must be sure to leave a little more white paper showing than you might at first think necessary or the garment could look lifeless and flat. Add ground color only for the pants at this stage.*

5. *Add the check detail to the pants using light, controlled pencil crayon strokes; you are aiming only to give a hint of the pattern. Use marker pens for accessories, hair, and skin tones, and correction pen to lend a crisp clarity to the polka-dotted bow tie.*

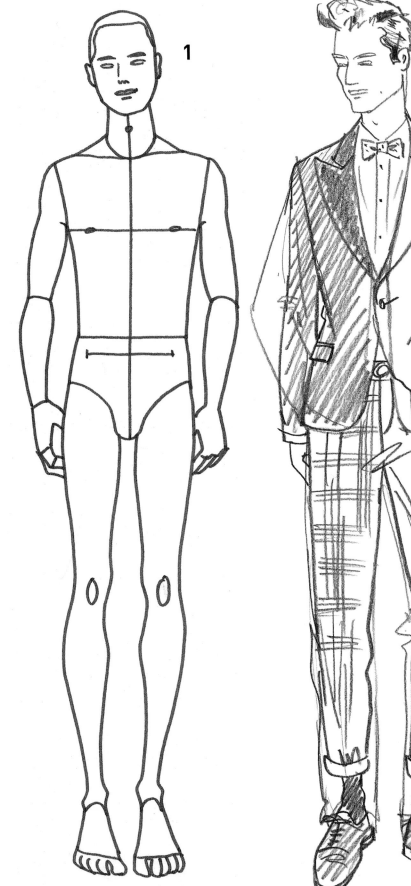

GLOSSARY

anatomy The physical structure of a person, animal, or other organism; also the branch of science that studies it. In fashion drawing, it is important to learn human anatomy in order to render it accurately.

base color A color used as a background over which other colors are painted in.

daylight bulb A light bulb that mimics the full spectrum of hues contained in sunlight, so that colors are seen as they would be outdoors in natural daylight.

dry materials Materials such as graphite, charcoal, china marker, conté pencils, and chalk or oil pastels, which can be used dry to render a drawing or illustration.

ephemera Objects of memorabilia, often written, printed, or painted, that are expected to have only short-term usefulness.

esoteric Requiring specialist knowledge, and so unlikely to be understood by most people.

found images Pictures used in illustration that were not produced with art in mind but which can be melded into an artwork or fashion, or simply used as inspiration.

implement In art, a tool used to draw or paint with, for example, a charcoal pencil or paintbrush.

inform To give an essential quality or principle to something.

life-drawing Drawing a picture from a live model rather than from a photograph or other image.

light box A flat box with a light inside and a translucent top that provides an evenly lit, flat surface for drawing or tracing.

masking fluid In artwork, a liquid applied with a brush to cover (or mask) areas of a surface on which paint is not wanted.

mood board A board decorated with materials such as found images, small objects, and fabric swatches, arranged to create the mood of something you wish to design.

nap The raised threads or hairs on the surface of a fabric and the direction in which they lie.

PR Public Relations—the maintenance of a favorable public image by a company, organization, group, or celebrity.

proportion In drawing, the correct or attractive relationship in size or shape between the parts of a subject, such as a figure.

render To represent or portray artistically—to draw or paint.

replicate To make an exact copy of something.

resist A substance applied as a coating to protect a surface during a process, for example, to stop paint from sticking.

silhouette A representation of someone showing the shape and outline only, not the details.

template A shaped piece of a material used as a pattern for a design.

utility The practical usefulness of an object.

warp	Lengthwise threads held in tension on a loom. Other threads are passed over and under these.	threads to make fabric on a loom.
		wet materials
weft	The threads that are drawn over and under the lengthwise warp	Materials such as watercolors, paints, inks, gouaches, markers, and spray adhesives that make up the artist's kit or set.

FURTHER READING

Angeletti, Norberto, and Alberto Oliva. *In Vogue: An Illustrated History of the World's Most Famous Fashion Magazine.* 2nd ed. New York: Rizzoli, 2012.

Baugh, Gail. *The Fashion Designer's Textile Directory: A Guide to Fabrics' Properties, Characteristics, and Garment-Design Potential.* 1st ed. Hauppauge, New York: Barron's Educational Series, 2011.

The Design Museum. *Fifty Dresses That Changed the World.* 1st ed. London: Conran, 2009.

Faerm, Steven. *Fashion Design Course: Principles, Practice, and Techniques: A Practical Guide for Aspiring Fashion Designers.* 1st ed. Hauppauge, New York: Barron's Educational Series, 2010.

Stalder, Erica. *Fashion 101: A Crash Course in Clothing.* San Francisco: Zest Books, 2008.

WEB SITES

Drawspace
www.drawspace.com
Art education site that offers 200 free downloadable lessons on all aspects of drawing, from sketching tools and techniques to drawing faces, figures, and fabrics.

Fashionista
www.fashionista.com
Keep up to date with the fashion illustration world, including information on the latest trends, designers, labels, blogs, and fashion shows. Also includes information on internships and careers in fashion.

Teen Vogue
www.teenvogue.com
This great source for design inspiration covers all the latest US and global teenage fashions. With features on catwalk fashion, everyday style, celebrity trends, and red-carpet looks.

Hilary Kidd
Brush and marker pen.

INDEX